RIVERSOFWOMEN
THE PLAY

RIVERSOFWOMEN
THE PLAY

by Shirley Bradley LeFlore

with photography by
Michael J. Bracey

2LEAF PRESS
NEW YORK
www.2leafpress.org

P.O. Box 4378
Grand Central Station
New York, New York 10163-4378
editor@2leafpress.org
www.2leafpress.org

2LEAF PRESS
is an imprint of the
Intercultural Alliance of Artists & Scholars, Inc. (IAAS),
a NY-based nonprofit 501(c)(3) organization that promotes
multicultural literature and literacy.
www.theiaas.org

Copyright © 2013 by Shirley Bradley LeFlore
Photography: Michael J. Bracey
Book design and layout: Gabrielle David

Library of Congress Control Number: 2013935748
ISBN-13: 978-0-9884763-7-0 (Paperback)

10 9 8 7 6 5 4 3 2 1

Published in the United States of America

First Edition | First Printing

2LEAF PRESS trade distribution is handled by University of Chicago Press / Chicago Distribution Center (www.press.uchicago.edu) 773.702.7010. Titles are also available for corporate, premium, and special sales. Please direct inquiries to the UCP Sales Department, 773.702.7248.

Special thanks to Donna Aiken who epitomizes the true meaning of "Rivers of Women." With much love, Gabrielle.

This play is dedicated
with love and admiration
to seven good women
MeMe, Dolly, Barbara Jane, Hope, Jacie, Lyah and Karen.

RIVERS OF WOMEN

In August 2011, *Rivers of Women* was produced as a staged reading at the Missouri History Museum in St. Louis for two sold out performances. The cast featured Kelly Jenkins and dancers, Nicole "Pinky" Thomas and Heather Himes. Due to popular demand, *Rivers of Women* was added to the 2012-2013 theater season at the Missouri History Museum for a six performance run. Below is the creative team and cast members for May 2013.

WRITTEN BY
Shirley Bradley LeFlore

DIRECTED BY
Lyah Beth LeFlore

EXECUTIVE PRODUCERS
Lyah Beth LeFlore
Ed Curtis
Takia "Tizzi" Green

PRODUCER
Marsha Cann

COMPOSER/PRODUCER
Alerica Anderson

ASSOCIATE PRODUCER
Theresa Anderson

PRODUCTION COORDINATOR
Celeste Porter

CHOREOGRAPHER
Nicole "Pinky" Thomas

DANCER
Brooke Boyd

CAST:
Woman #1 – Leah Stewart
Woman # 2 – Rochelle "Coco Soul" Walker
Woman # 3 – Adrianne Felton
Woman #4 – Olivia Neal
*Woman #5 – (Guest Star) Monifah Carter

MUSICIANS
Alerica Anderson – Piano, Vocals
David Jackson – Percussions
Grover Stewart, Jr. – Drums
John King – Bass

CONTENTS

i

SUITE III: LOVE

SUITE IV: HEALING

BEHIND THE SCENES

FOREWORD

Give me rivers
Rivers of my ancestors
Give me the real story
Herstory
The strength of my strong
The poetry in my poem
The rhythm in my dance
The musik in my song
To remember not to forget the journey of my sheroes
To keep the light burning inside so strong
Like fire shut up in my bone
So I can keep their breathprints in my bosom
And their words on my tongue…

RIVERS OF WOMEN is a collection of original pieces from my repertoire of works including the iconic title poem "Rivers of Women." The poems within this book, interwoven in the deeply personal and intimate narrative, are snap shots of the women's voices that have influenced my life, coming from a St. Louis state of mind. Some in ear shot of their tales and stories, others, my imagination took flight just listening to them.

Growing up in St. Louis, or as my Grandmother, whom we called MeMe, use to say, "The Big River City Town, with its people a 'lil bit country and a 'lil bit citified," it was fascinating. I experienced memorable seasons and learned to appreciate their fullness. From winters, cold with snow and ice, spring with its dandelions and clover spreading a sunny smile on the neighborhood lawns; summers so hot you knew it was gonna be as the song goes, "a hot time in 'ole town tonight" and the quick bereavement of autumn under raspberry skys, and trees get to shedding its green, getting naked, ready for its white and icy winter dress.

I was born in 1940, and during that time St. Louis was known for it's industry and manufacturing. This was also during the time there was a wave of the second migration from the south and southeast Missouri. African Americans were coming to a segregated St. Louis, sometimes called "upsouth," based on this river town's proximity to the Mason Dixon line.

As a young girl, I recall the streetcars running east and west on Franklin Avenue, starting at the Mississippi, merging onto Easton Avenue, running all the way to the Wellston Loop (now named Martin Luther King, Jr. Boulevard). This was the main vein that traveled through the African American community, and urban life was abuzz. Merchants from furniture and clothing stores, to independently owned markets, fruit and vegetable stands, drugstores, and 5 and 10 cent stores, lined the blocks.

It was a time that black businesses bloomed and black women entrepreneurs emerged. Entrepreneurs like my mother who owned a local beauty shop with her sisters, and eventually moved it into our home. I spent a great deal of time in her beauty shop as a child, and it allowed me to be exposed to a diverse group of colored women. I listened to their tales and stories, and the various textures of their language, and was impressed by their stylish clothing. This was where the women gathered.

They also gathered in our home. But instead of just the beauty shop patrons, it was the women in my family. They gathered there regularly, talking women's talk. From family secrets, church news and gossip, to men, their dreams, loves, and who was doing what to who. Children weren't allowed to be around, but I would be in another room playing jacks, or with my dolls, or coloring, slyly listening with one ear to these conversations that danced across the kitchen table.

Church was no exception, either. I would find entertainment listening to the delicious conversations the old ladies would have. When I rode the streetcar or bus, and overheard the whispering conversations women exchanged, I made sure I was within earshot. I would often make up plays in the backyard about these very women. My plays evolved into the discovery of my love for writing poetry.

I could also play the piano. My sister, Barbara Jane and I were both musical prodigies. So I would play the piano and speak the words I wrote, and close my eyes and see those women again and again, this time hearing their voices even louder. Their spirits had come alive. In reflection, I think St. Louis women have always represented spirit, style, class, and strength.

These images are told through the poetry that, as a young girl, I wrote in my imagination. I watched black women, blu, blak, and hi-yellow, old, young, tall and lanky, short and stout, on the streetcars and buses, tired from doing day work in Ladue or University City for rich white folk, carrying bags of groceries, or all dressed up Sunday mornin' shine, with their husbands and babies held close. I smelled the sweetness of toilette water, dabbed behind their ears.

I even dreamt about these women as I lay on my back in the grass in the vast lushness of St. Louis' famous Forest Park. My parents took us there on Sundays in the summertime. Back then, black families could sleep outside in the park. As I starred into the thick, black sky, smattered with millions of white glistening stars, I imagined those women again. I saw them on back porches, fanning themselves, sippin' on fresh tart lemonade, keepin' cool in the shade. These same women, mocha-cinnamon-milky-skinned, were writing their own reflections on napkins in the tavern, or on the backs of brown paper bags. When they were sad about something, happy about something else, or as they daydreamed about lovers they had, lost, or didn't have.

They wrote Jesus poems, poems for Sunday school, Easter, Christmas and Mother's Day. They also wrote about their children, husbands, boyfriends and girlfriends. They wrote a lot about their dreams and wishes and fantasies.

As I got older and developed, throughout high school, college, and into adulthood, I continued writing my poetry. Once I had a family of my own, late nights, when the house was sleeping I would have my writing time. I had found my true voice, and expressing myself through words became second nature to me. With the emergence of the Civil Rights Movement, my art began to come full circle, and I started performing my poetry publicly with musicians, dancers and visual artists.

I remember vividly, one setting near the Mississippi, or what we called that Ole Muddy Miss, I began to envision a multitude of women coming onto the levee out of the river. These women had different faces and voices, and they were different colors, singing a coming home chant. It was a powerful experience and thrust the birth of the poem, "Rivers of Women." In the original piece, I was able to profile the many women I had met over the years, throughout my life. Women I worked with, counseled with, family, friends. Some I knew and some I'd yet to meet, and women that lived inside of me.

I was reminded of my mother and how she loved "her girls," and of my grandmother, MeMe. She was indeed grande, and she wasn't just my grandmother, but a queen, regal, royal, rare. She was always dressed, always dressed impeccably, never without her hat or silk headscarf tied to the side. On sunny days she was never without her parasol. Her wise insight stitched under her feet, from slavery, Jim Crow, segregation, over oceans and rivers, celebrating women.

All these years later after writing the poem "Rivers of Women," I can still hear music moving these women to dance in the street, in the club, in the church, in the living room, dancing under my skin. So, with the encouragement of my youngest daughter, who has followed in my footsteps as a writer, I decided to wrap the piece around a collection of poems and stuff them in some other woman's bosom. The overwhelmingly positive response from the stage play adaptation of *Rivers of Women,* along with the other women-centered poems from my vault, has allowed me to see the fruits of my pen's labor.

As women, we stand on the shoulders of women who have been great throughout history, our grandmothers, our great grandmothers, our mothers, our aunts. The play, *Rivers of Women,* represents all the different women who have lived inside of me at some point in time, and I think both men and women can take something of significance away after reading these pages. For men, it will give them a little bit better understanding of the complexity of womanhood.

For women, a tear falls. It opens up a greater insight of women that they can discover their humanity, their womanness, but they can also be entertained and informed. So to readers, be more aware about how you feel about the women in you, and men, about the women in your life! ☻

— Shirley Bradley LeFlore
with Lyah Beth LeFlore
St. Louis, Missouri
March 2013

SUITE I:THE SPIRIT

GIVE ME RIVERS

Opening musical interlude. Woman Nos. 1, 2, 3 and 4 emerge from backstage and sing a medley of gospel songs for the praise and worship opening of the play. As the final song fades, the Women freeze hands to the side and begin to recite the first poem.

Woman No. 1

give me rivers
rivers of my sheros that flowed down thru
the ages of my bloodline
rich like pot liquor
the breathprints of their season

the echos of their names
the strength of my strong
the story my song
their names stitched under the
    souls of my feet

(whispered) harriet...meme...dolly...
i stand on their shoulders
steady and unmovable
i am the continum of their journey
rivers and rivers and rivers of women
    hush...hush, hush, somebody's callin my name
    hush...hush, hush, somebody's callin my name
    hush...hush, hush, somebody's callin my name

The Women sing, then stage goes dark. Woman Nos. 1, 3, 4 and Dancer No. 2 exit stage. Dancer No. 1 performs dance interlude. Woman No. 2 takes center stage.

WOMAN I AM

Woman No. 2

woman I am
the symbol of love
the channel of creation
the vibration of peace
the anger of storms
the pain of suffering
woman i am natural to the...bone

Stage goes dark. Segue into upbeat, soul-filled gospel transition. Lights up. Dance interlude and performance by chorus. Woman Nos. 1 and 3 re-enter carrying fans. The Women are seated as if in church pews and fan themselves, while doing a slow church sway.

THE WOMEN GATHER

Woman No. 1

The women gather
like painted brides/a tapestry
of eyes/hands/knees/hearts like open baskets
pieces of their peace/fragments of their dreams
snatches of their lives/with their mothers
mothers rhythms/visions/breathprints/wrapped in their bosom

Woman No. 2

The women gather
dropping tongues in terra-cotta bowls
with their bibles and charms/bluz, boogie, herbs, oils, and curls
seeing eyes and gospel pearls/heady laughter/lies and tears
rolling like Jordan/prayers, rituals, and folktales
stuffed between their teeth/a bloodline rich and mahogany

Woman No. 3

The women gather
mothers, daughters, sisters, wives, and sweethearts
grannies and aunt sister bell and hoochies with their hellhounds
and hollars/their children and men/lost lovers/lifted
leftover/forever and lasting with skeletons/secrets/gri-gri
and hush-hush folded in little bitty pieces

Woman No, 4

The women gather
knitting hands/re-stitching their lives
reconnecting the circle
piecing the quilt to keep us warm
from generations for generations and generations to come…

All of the Women take chairs and exit off stage. Music up and under. Gospel infused music bleeds into a jazzy interlude performed by Dancer No. 1. Woman Nos. 1, 2 and 3 enters stage.

I HAVE KNOWN WOMEN

Woman No. 1

I HAVE KNOWN WOMEN/RIVERS OF WOMEN
Blu/blck/tan/high yella/blu-vein women rivercrossing women/waters
deep as the nile/mississippi as mud/seaboard and island ocean
women/women who ride the waves and balance the tide/swimming
women/waterwalking women/treading waters/floating/going w/
the flow women/backstroking/jellyfishing/mud crawling
women/i know women who drown/sinking women who sleep
at the bottom of the waters

I HAVE KNOWN WOMEN
flying women-hawkeye and eaglewing who spread/stir the nest/
strike the wind and soar/women who strap mercury around their
ankles/making airborne feet/flying women who fly off the handle/
up against brick walls and breakwing/women who fly non-stop
w/earlobes/elbows/toenails and tongues like flying saucers/fly
by night women swiftwing and blind as a bat at high noon/
straighten up and fly right women/women with magic
underwing/i know women of wonder w/moon eyes

8

Woman No. 2

I HAVE KNOWN WOMEN

bold/brave/brass and sassy women/cinnamon breath and whispering
smiles/women w/custom designed life lines that make beauty a new
face/women w/struggling wrists/jagged edges/women w/life
lines that read like worn-out road maps/i know women sweetbread
and sourdough/rainbow wrapped

I HAVE KNOWN WOMEN

women who see/who lay a 3rd eye on evil dare it to move and make
it sink in a blink/women who hear/who put ear to a stone/
x-ray a moan/hear a cry before a tear drops/women w/keen nostrils
who smell shit before it stinks/women reminiscing and ruminating
on the rudiments of roots and the source of natures remedies/
diviners/root women

Woman No. 3

I HAVE KNOWN WOMEN
troubled women w/sacks/satchels/bags and bundles of trouble
women who serve trouble on a platter and chaos for desert
women who carry trouble like a bone/w/tall tales and who shot
john about other women/lying women/women who sneaky pete
at the backdoor and cheat in the frontroom/see sawin/hem-hawin/
double-tongue/lying women/thieving women who steal
your money/your honey and unlaugh your funny

I HAVE KNOWN WOMEN
women peachcheeks/maybelline/ruby lips/
swingin hips/face in paint/full of haints/women who sleep in your backpocket/
wear you down to a nub/run you ragged as sauerkraut
women who dare "DO RIGHT" to come round their stoop and make
"GOOD STUFF" tuck tail and haul ass/I know women who turn
peace to piss and put a hellhound at risk

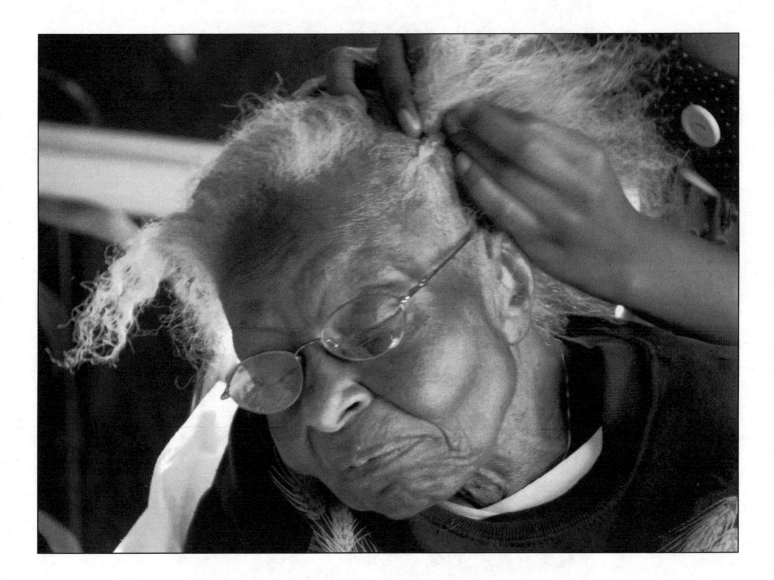

Woman No. 4

I HAVE KNOWN WOMEN

dancing women/be-bop and shushu feet women who re-bop
a jitterbug real sweet/package a hukka-buck and sell it/
hip-hoppin/bop a boogie woggie stompin women/women holy
rolling/dancing w/jesus/two stepping w/the devil/rocking w/the wind
women/drumfeet-bare and sturdy/dancing women
dancing the wrinkles out of their brows/bed and their head/
making spirit rise/passion/snatches a jellyroll and a boody-grind
like an electric slide women who point ballet/boogaloo/dance
the nutcracker between the cracks-in her life

Woman No. 2

I HAVE KNOWN WOMEN

healing women/spirit women/of vision/women who beat a dream
comin true/peacekeeping women sun-sipping/women who light up dark corners
and dingy hearts/women who put a move on the fog/knees of harmony
and smooth teeth/divas and doers/righteous women of purpose/substance/
w/music/wordwalkers between the foot of the mountain and the mouth
of the sun/lovesowers and seedplantingwomenbirthing and bridging/praying
women/standingground women/traveling light/w/good vibes laughing women
who be merry w/tears that turn crystal

Women in unison

I KNOW THESE WOMEN

these mothers and daughters and lovers and wives/these sisters/grannies/queenies
and hoochies/these women who make women to make women/to make men/
I know these women

Woman No. 1

I HAVE KNOWN WOMEN/RIVERS OF WOMEN

blu/blk/tan/high-yella/blu-vein women
knitting hands/collectingeyes/ribbons/photographs/hairclippings
poems and stories/stringing pearls and parables/tears and smiles/
gathering picnic baskets/silk gloves/birthmarks/teacups and ashes/
pickin the flowers/snatching the breathprints of women past/writing
a song called – WOMEN/RIVERS OF WOMEN

Women in unison.

As the Women speak in unison, sometimes in sync, sometimes randomly, sounding like echoes, repeated 6 times.

RIVERS/WOMEN OF RIVERS
RIVERS OF WOMEN/WOMEN

The Women freeze and Woman No. 2 moves center stage and sings. As the music fades, the Women exit the stage. Dance interlude performed by Dancer No. 1. Fade out.

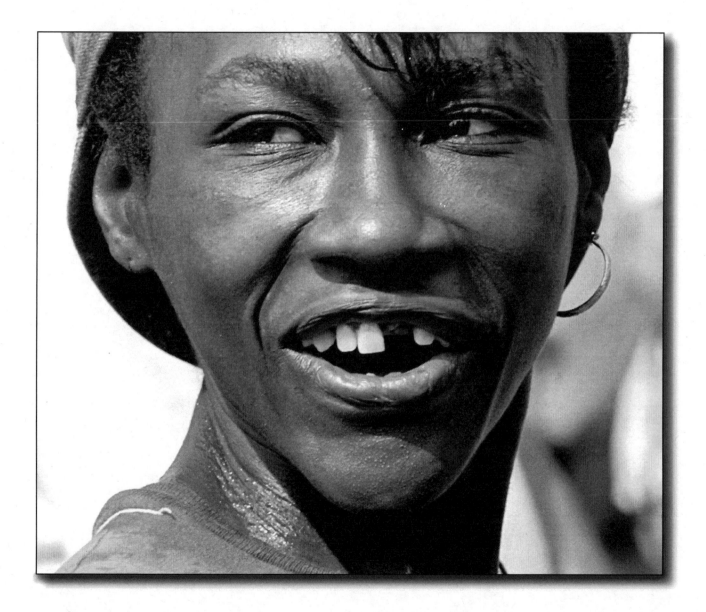

SUITE II:THE SOUL

WE BE DOLLY'S GIRLS

Lively blues-infused music up full as the beauty shop scene is being created before the audience's eyes. Women No. 1 and Woman No. 2 return to the stage with chairs and sit in them, as Dancer No. 2. follows with a handheld mirror and pressing comb, pretending to do each Woman's hair through dance. The Women engage in inaudible chatter and laughter.

Woman No. 1

We be Dolly's girls
Silk, sassy w/good sense & classy
Love passed down in the bloodline
Rich like pot-liquor

Women in unison

DOLLY'S GIRLS

Woman No. 2

We know how to shine fine like elderberrywine
We know how to laugh, smile, cry and scream
Act dignified, uppity, sometimes grumpy
Act-up and out, in and out, country and citified
A little-bit crazy, a little-bit sane
Mix it all up, mix it all down with a dream and wish
We be a special dish, the bold, the beautiful, the brown
Some short, some tall, some skinny, others a little too round

Women in unison

DOLLY'S GIRLS

Woman No. 1

We know how to boogie with the boogieman
We know how to stomp with the devil
Sing with Angels with/out a cracked note
We know how to beat them odds – dance with God

Music out. The Women and Dancer freeze. The Women face the audience.

Women in unison

We be Dolly's girls
Love passed down in the bloodline
Rich like pot-liquor

BLESSED/REDRESSED/AND/FREE
A REFLECTION OF HER
LOVE-SUPREME

The Women hold their places still seated, Dancer No. 2 exits. Dancer No. 1 enters stage.

SISTAS

Woman No. 1 and Woman No. 2 in unison

We have sang/solo/duo/trio
cried/moaned/lied and laughed
together

Woman No. 1

We have done the cat-eye
scratch in the night
holler'd/screamed like
a snaggle-tooth hyena
and fought like fire and woke-up
in the smile of a new sun

Woman No. 1 and Woman No. 2 in unison

together

24

Woman No. 2

We pieced together our dreams
witnessed stuff fall apart at the seams
kept sacred our secrets/being who we be
earned degrees/helped each other in dis-ease
choked back life's tears/untangled our fears
fell down busted-up and scar'd our knees
got up and started all over again

Woman No. 1 and Woman No. 2 in unison

together

The Women face each other and clasp hands.

Woman No. 2

Crashed hormones and tracked hellhounds
witnessed the miracle of birth touched
the pain of death and the ugly of sick
felt the beauty of god's spirit
been redeemed, been born again

Woman No. 1 and Woman No. 2 in unison

together

Woman No. 1

Tasted love and loss and memories
felt the cooling board of our mother
the winding sheet of our father
and the smootheyes of each other

Woman No. 1 and Woman No. 2 in unison

together

Short pause before continuing in unison

SISTAS
Discovered our beauty/our strong/our talents/ourselves
we are love-rich and mahogany/we are friends
we are sistas

Woman Nos. 1, 2, 3 and 4 sings and then exit stage.

WILDFLOWERS

Music cue and Woman Nos. 1, 2, 3 and 4 enter center stage and sing as Woman No. 4 speaks.

Wildflowers
A flower grows /in beauty wild
seed of nature's soul /wildflowers grow
heaven's tears and sunstruck skys /
wicked winds /a breath of storms
under winters' gray or autumns' raspberry clouds

A flower born /laughs, lives, dances, sings, dies
returns /blossoms /again lives
nurtured by nature

B'tween green weeds and sweet grass /meadows
and fields /clover and brush like a woman tale
spinning her colorful journey swirling and
skirting pinksweets and poppies /primrose and
buttercups /chamomile and chicory /blu flax and
baby breath purple cones dandelions and daffodils /
catchflies and a dragon fly among a basket of
gold (marigolds) / Nurtured by nature

Wild as blackeyed suzies /scarlet yarrows, morning
glories /wild blu iris / Johnny jump-ups /ox-eyed
daisies soothing as lavender hyssop and creeping
zenias growing wild along roadsides and byways
highways /country trails and iron rails
                    Nurtured by nature

A colorama spray growing /beauty wild like
a ladywomanflowergirl /bending /swaying /face-up
and bowing /standing tall in the earthtones
and greens in chaos and calm /growing
                    Wildflowers … … …

Dancer and Woman No. 1 exit as Woman Nos. 2 and 3 remain on stage to perform song, and then exit, lights dim.
Intermission 15 minutes

SUITE III:LOVE

QUIET STORM (HE CAME)

Woman No. 3 emerges. Music up full and under. Dancer No. 1 performs.

Woman No. 3

He
Came by night
Moved inside me with a pocket full of rainbows...
He
Came with the holy ghost
To chase the devil away
Walked like hieroglyphics
Thru my temple

He came
Writing the psalms of ancient pyramids
On the walls of my soul
Singing a 2000 year old anthem
Making me song

He came
A soft sculpturer designing still visions
Draped my body velvet
Stretched me out on a canvas
Of cool waters

He came
Speaking in tongues to my spirit
Crested a star in my forehead
Sealed it with his sign
Moved his sun around my moon

Made the rains gather at the river
Of my thighs
And my navel full
With sacred oil
Giving birth
To a real love ritual

He came
To baptize my history
Purge my future

He
Came by night
A quietstorm…

Silence. Dancer freezes. Spotlight on Woman No. 2.

USED TO BE

Woman No. 2

I could sing of memories
And once upon a time
And
Tender that crossed my heart
And
Eyes… (pause)

Silence. Dancer No. 1 inrterprets pause.

...And used to be sighs
That cried between my thighs
And laid hands on my mind
And
Kept me high
Naturally
But...But...But
I would only be reminded of
You
Gone with the wind...

Woman No. 3 and Dancer No. 1 exit stage. Musical interlude moves into a moody blues feel. We imagine a tenament/apartment building setting, with each woman looking out of her window. Lights up full on Woman No. 1 as she begins to roll up her hair for what we assume is getting ready to go to a party.

I HEAR YOU COMIN'

Woman No. 1

I hear you comin'
Lightfoot and hummin'
I hear you comin'
Like an uptown blues
Wearing them woreout downtownshoes

I hear you

Like a rock rolling stonesmooth
Checking out the vibes
Eyeballing the signs
Trying to see blind

I hear you comin'
Lightfoot and hummin'

With a windcharming angel folded under your wings
Some leftover dreams
With the earth folkdancin'
Circling your feet
I hear you

Silent like night and easy like evening
Strumming your pain like a stringmissin' guitar
Guarding your star

I hear you comin'

songwalking me with a leconic sound
eyepicking my waters like a juice harp
trying to play me

I hear you comin'
Lightfoot and hummin'
Like a hush hush hobo
Working your boogie juggie mojo

I hear you

Moonstroking me like gold
Sipping off my city soul
Musing the soft in my bend
But a countryriver woman ain't go no end

I hear you
I hear you comin'
Lightfoot and hummin'

Now you can go on 'bout your bizness!

Woman No. 1 puts the last roller in her hair. Lights out. Lights up on Woman No. 2. Music changes to upbeat tempo. She is stirring a pot on the stove.

SATURDAYNITE HOUSERENT

Woman No. 2

Saturday nite and the lites are low
The music is loud and the lovin' is slow
Possum got tators and the coon got gravy
Crowders in the pot and I like mine hot
Come on round to the back of my flat open the door when I throw the latch
You can't be jivin' when the lites flick on
Cause we got some juju and a barr'l of corn

Betty and mable and marylu
e.j. and willie gon be there too

dice'll be rolling big peal be callin'
if your luck ain't good you can still be ballin'

cause short dress chicks and big apple dudes
be gittin' down with the houchee koo

look out for shortee and his 45
with annimae glued to his side

he gon start showin out trying to be cool
watch him dare Harvey to step on his shoes

check Chlotille when she gets real loud
and screams on Leroy "git your hand from under my dress 'fore I get my razor and sample
your chest!"

Muddywaters be duellin' with Memphis Slim
While Lit'nin Hopkins and Howlin Wolf be waitin' to take over again

You can look for Hattimae to get real hi

And her ole man Curtis gon be peepin' sly out the corner of his eye
To make sure Juanita gon be standin' by
Dorothy's gon commence to pullin up her dress
And Roosevelt gon have to give her some fist to make her rest

Way in the background, cutting thru the noise
Sarah's gon be scattin shoo bop de du sha ba be du dattin'
And Big Daddy Fats gon sho nuf be cattin'

Yeh – soulville baby at the gloryhole
Put your chump change in your pocket
Park your coup de ville and lock it

Saturday nite and the lites are love the music is loud and the lovin' is slow
Possums got tators and the coon got gravy
Crowders in the pot and I like mine hot

Lights out on Woman No. 2. Lights up on Woman No. 4 sitting on a chair turned backwards. As she straddles the chair, she gracefully relaxes her arms over the back of the chair. She smiles, taking in her surroundings. Casually, she begins to apply red lipstick and adjust the flower in her hair.

MEN HAVE BUTTERED MY BREAD

Woman No. 5

Men have buttered my bread on both-sides
Wined me, dined me
Took me to the ball
Loved me like Sunday morning church
Glory all the week
Bathed me in sunshine
Almost melted me blind
Touched me gently with their minds
Laid hands on my soul
Some lasted thru the cold
Coming full circle in July

Men have buttered my bread on both-sides
Wined me, dined me
Took me to the ball
Some flew me around their world
1/2 inch short of getting back to my own
Laid hands on my secrets
Made my nature high
My temperature rise
Turned my whisper to a holler, please!
And laugh between my knees
Some fried me, tried me, burned me
Washed me, wrung me, hung me out to dry
Some disappeared, left me tripping, tipping
into darkness

Some sent me to the school of hard knocks, rocks in my bed
That almost settled in my head

Men have buttered my bread on both sides
Wined me, dined me
Took me to the ball – showed me life the paradise/life the paradox
But they still be
My sweet inspirations

Woman No. 5 turns her chair around and sits, straddling her chair with her back to the audience frozen in a provacative pose. Music cues up. The imaginary walls of each apartment disappears and before our eyes the party comes to life. Woman No. 1 and Woman No. 2 come back to life with their bodies swaying to the music. Woman No. 3, Dancer No. 1 and Dancer No. 2 enter the stage and join the party, swaying to the music.

PUT YA HAINTS ON ME

Woman No. 5 joined by Dancer No. 1 and Dancer No. 2

Put ya haints on me
Put summa dat goobie dus alroun' my feet
Pluck a lock of mah hair – wear it ever'where
Wring a chick'nz neck til it hoop
Sprinkle seasalt/under mah stoop
Criss cross me wid a blk catz bone
Lawd lawd make me wanna stay home

Woman No. 5 continues joined by Dancer No. 1

Sorcerize me if you must
Work yo roots sho-nuf
Cuz I like the way you do my stuff

Ya makes my juice box run
Like hot butter'd rum
Ya love me so good
I wanna skip jump & run
Makes me def blind & dumb

Put ya haints on me

Woman No. 5 continues joined by Dancer No. 2

Squeeze me like ya do that eagle on a dolla
Take ma whisper to a holla/
Turn ma minutes to an hour/
Increase me to the 3rd power

Put ya haints on me

Sorcerize me if ya must
Work ya roots sho nuf
Cuz I like the way you do mah stuff

When you see me comin /click ya heels 3 times
Wid a grigri rhyme /but dontcha make no wish
When ya see me comin /beat ya breast 3 times
And make a mojo sign /but dontcha make no wish
B'cause ya fix won't mix /on a Creole woman fish

Gon & put ya haints on me

Now, ya kin snake hip me and tare up ya face
Ya know I lov being yo amazin' grace

So re nu me do me wid ya hoodoo bluz
Wid a hex ana spell an sum duji ju ju

Gon & put ya haints on me

Woman No. 5 continues joined by Dancer No. 1

I won't burn no candle drink no frog-eye tea
Put no bunkleberry leaves up my sleeves
Kiss my elbo or hoot oil my knees
I won't bathe in no sage
carry no cloves for 3 days
And I won't search for no conjure man wid no lousanna hand
To take em off

Jus rememba who you dowhenyoudodahoodoo
Cuz you may be tha who/who be hoodoo'd

Stage goes black.

SUITE IV:HEALING

LOVE POEM

Percussion interlude. Lights up.
Woman No. 4

I am a love poem
Let me be

I am not light
I am not heavy
I am neither rite nor wrong
Jus'
Consider me
The balance

I sit low in the corner of your left eye
And see inside the depth of high in your right
I stand in the center of space
And confirm the substance of time

I am a love poem
Let me be

I am tired
By your lamenting

Tired of you trying to direct my course
Falsely accuse me, explain me, blame me
For your own short comings
And to be very frank

I am tired of you always trying to kill yourself in my name
I am the living
Call me love

You assault me
Throw me against stonewalls, stomp on me
Maul me with your knees
Squash me between your toes
Spit on me

Then say
Love is painful

You insult me
Put me down
Shake me down
Call me weak
Starve me like hungry
Let me go naked

Woman No. 5 exits. Woman No. 3 and Dancer No. 2 enters stage.

WHEN A SISTERWOMANPOET PRAYS

Women No. 3 (Dancer No. 2 interprets in dance.)

When a sisterwomanpoet prays
She prays w/a glass eye
Sees double w/single vision
Connects chains of light

When a sisterwoman prays
Muse and meditate
Fuse spirit and soul
Collects the higher power

She strips doubt naked
Kicks fear in the ass
Assassinates evil
Turns insight out

She touches the all-sum of god
Releases ego/transcends/expands
Breaks bread w/the universe
The artist paints her angel

When a sisterwoman prays
She be gettin results

Woman No. 3 and Dancer No. 2 exit stage. Music transitions into the Women singing offstage. Woman No. 2 and Woman No. 1 emerge and stand parallel to each other.

TIME/WISE FOR ME ME

Woman No. 2

She saw tomorrow
N/time-woman/time-mother/time
Like her mother's mothers before
Mother Mary

She saw tomorrow
W/a righteous eye/an ear w/an echo and a 7th sense
She cd see the sunrise in the sparrow's eye
Hear day-light fall into the arms of night
Feel the moon creep up and rescue the dark
She saw tomorrow
N/time/woman time/mother time

She knew time
Like she knew Jesus
Like she knew Joshua and her 13 babies

She knew time
She cd feel it
Like the long dark fingers of her ancestors
Feel it like dusk breathing a hush hush

She knew time
She cd smell it/smell it like trouble
Like a fresh storm brewing

She knew time
She cd taste it/like the honey in a woodwater rock
Like the red-clay in the bottoms that she dusted
Her lips w/now and again

Woman No. 1

She knew time
Like the inside of her palms
Like the leaves that settled in her teacup
Like the crystal in her children's eye
Like the fear in her man's sweat

She knew time
W/every seed she carried and everyone she buried
W/every ear she pierced and every strand of hair
She cut on the new moon

She saw tomorrow
N/time seeing-eye time
Like the signs

She knew
The peculiar witchcraft of oppression like
The terror of a scream wrapped tightly in a sigh
On the secret of a moan/a prayer w/out a word

She knew
Life's only promise to be death and struggle's
Greatest invention to be victory

Woman No. 2

She knew time to be a matter/of/time
That all be appointed by time
That ungodly deeds would be done in the name of god
That freedom like truth/crushed/wd always rise
That the tears of the unloved wd come back/turned to blood
That the innocent like the guilty wd have to drink
That rage be the broken mirror of peace

She knew time to be a matter/of/time
That unholy institutions to be unnecessary to be holy whole
That the vanity of man's law to be lawless
That man like the monkey wd cut shines and capers
Footslip and be swallowed by folly and eat dung like hamburger

Woman No. 1

She knew time to be a matter/of/time
She knew time like the wind changes but never cease
Breaking out & up & clean for good smelling
That time to be different from times
That religion to be different from righteousness
That every spirit is not spiritual

She knew time like the wind changes but never cease
She knew
That man wd try to hold time/try time/record time/mark time/
Change time/ignore time/try to fold time in little bitty pieces
But time like the mind changes but never cease
Time Time Time   is just a matter/of/time

62

Woman No. 2

She saw tomorrow/n'/yesterday
N' time/womantime
Like her mothers/mothers/mothers
B'fore her mother Mary

She was like time stubborn & unmovable
A heritage
Singing in the bloodline – like gospel
A revival
Passing down time/rich like pot liquor
She was spirit/was time/was song/was poem
Healing – mending the circle
& like motherearth
Can't no grave hold a seeing-eye-spirit/time/womansong

Music transition. Woman No. 1 and Woman No. 2 cross each other. Woman No. 1 stands in front of her pedestal, Woman No. 2 sits on her pedestal. Woman No. 3 and Woman No. 4 emerge and sit on their pedestals. Dancer No. 1 emerges to interpret their words.

BROKEN N' PARTS

Woman No. 1

broke n' parts
across bloodline and geography
the women gather/coming in from their winter
threads of yesterday's fabric
like a tattered dress that once
danced a full circle/

they come
w/tongues stuffed in their pockets
stories and tales swimming in the pools of their eyes
smiles of the lie/songs sleeping behind the mask
tears dried-up/dirges of lost grandmothers/fathers
who wore them like briefs/daughters who broke out of their mothers
womb running/sons who forgot to remember them/ditties
and dirges whispering under their skin/
they come

Woman No. 2

pieces of their lives balled up
in their fist/fragments of their dreams/
their houses/photographs/broken hearts and china/
fingernails like frayed paper flowers
they come like broke down promises
once firm breast fallen/the smell of love like
clabber milk/their rapture ruptured
they come
collecting shadows
picking up eyes and breathprints
that hang over their shoulders/coming
like a march wind breaking
against their backs
like the sun creeping thru the cracked skies
spirits rising from the ashes
they come

Woman No. 4

picking memories from b'tween their teeth
tracing the trail of their tears
and once upon a time laughter
rediscovering their voices
reinventing themselves
fresh dancing
busting loose/breaking bread
and silence/tale spinning and
story swapping/shaking the wrinkles out of their tongues
piecing and patching/reconnecting their broken circles
w/healing threads
they come
full circle

The dancer exits. The Women freeze.

HEALING

Woman No. 3

Bear my wind cracked song
Wounded on the second bar
In the throat of your silver trumpet
Play me a getting up morning
A full heart melody
Fold my broken wing inside your bosom
With a healing score
Dance me upstream
A golden salmon sonnet
An angel overture
On a long silk-tone
Make the music honeysweet
A clear note
And let me soar

THE CAGED BIRD SINGS

Woman No. 4

I got 2 wings to cover my face
2 wings to cover my feet
and 2 wings to fly away

The caged bird always sings
God gave him a song and six wings
A firesong
Last time and the next time too
A firesong, burning for joy
Yearning for peace
Firesong, struggling for food and shoes
Begging nomore dues that don't ever get paid
The caged bird always sings
Black crow-caws like a mocking birds repeat
o-hear freedom ring – far in a distant

anybody know what bird be caged

cagedbird be black as the color of some trulove's hair
but he got wings
he got eyes that cry in the wilderness, "feed the sparrows"
but he got wings
cagedbird be read in lifebooks that don't ever get read
but he got wings
the bird looks back 400 years and sees 400 years hence
and screech, Jesus wuz a man just like my daddy
and sometimes my mamma

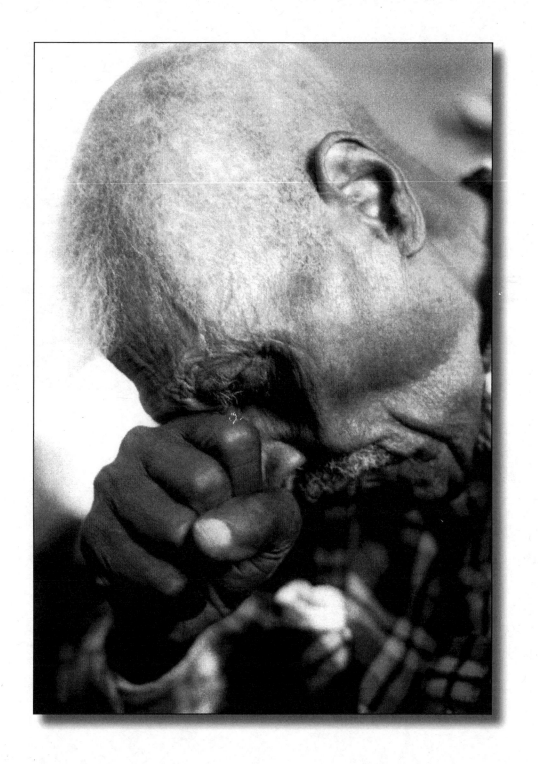

he be colored ibo-ebony, sundawnbronze and tallered yellow
with a black grandma
the cagedbird always sings

god gave him a song and six wings
the bird just wants to trade freedoom for freedom
sing his song and use his six wings

I got 2 wings to cover my face
2 wings to cover my feet
and 2 wings to fly away

Music interlude. Woman No. 5 sings. Woman Nos. 2, 3, 4 and 5 exit stage. Woman No. 1 grabs a music stand and places it center stage, stands behind it and speaks.

I WOKE-UP THIS MORNING

Woman No. 1

I woke-up this morning
More than something on my mind
Woke up
Under a New Orleans sky
Raspberry dust crawling the green
Where clouds sweat / blossoms scent sweet
Voodoo walks and a mojo talks where
Cooling boards like wooden hands lay slavery drybones
Wrapped in black winding sheets /someday to rise again
W/nommo swansongs or dirges black and blue
I woke-up

Woke up w/more than something on my mind/me-jesus-chicago
Got out my traveling shoes
Woke-up/ready to MOVE ON UP A LITTLE HIGHER
Unhitched my mule/strapped on my gospel boots
Bus ticket in my hand/freedom spiritpraise in my bosom
The gift of song in the throat of my soul- don't you know
Harmony unstrung and a melody unbent/going up yonder
God made me song/and bid me sing a lift everyvoice song
A borned again song/my hope built on nothing less
Than faith and righteousness
I woke-up/w/more than something on my mind/me-jesus-chicago

God made me song /bid me sing
The Amazing of God's Grace
Soon one morning I put on my traveling shoes
To walk all over this land
From the Mississippi bottoms
To England's kingdoms

God made me song/made me free to sing
Uplifting the lowly/humbling the boldly
I woke up this morning/the song
God song/a peace song/a gittin up song/a love song
I woke up this morning singing/singing/singing
And
MY SOUL LOOK BACK IN WONDER 'HOW I GOT OVER ... ...
...

Woman No. 1 exits stage. Dancer No. 1 enters stage.

THE DANCER

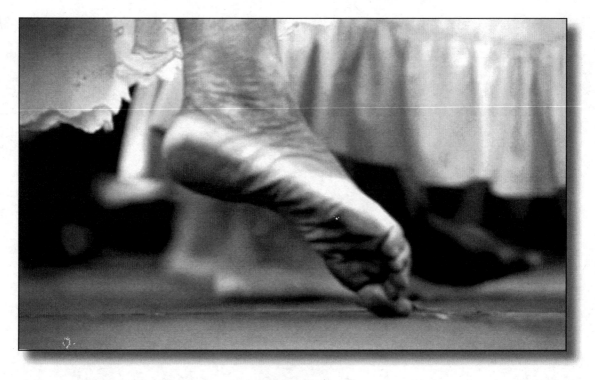

Woman No. 1 (Dancer No. 1 performs dance)

She comes from the sage garden
With the rhythm of Mutima dancing under skin
Whispering breathprints out of Africa/spirit songs
Singing under the soul of her feet
Drum voices speaking in mahogany tongues calling
Nations of talking feet/river dancing spirits
Choreostories reconnecting our bloodline in black gold

Woman No. 1 exits stage. African drummers emerge and play interlude. All of the Women enter center stage and hold hands.

POEM FOR A BLACK WOMAN

Woman No. 1

I house the legend of Mutima
The heartbeat of the earth
I am the offspring of the moon and the sun
Thrust from the energy of Africa
I am the Black Woman

Woman No. 2

I am the symbol of love
The channel of creation
The vibration of peace
The anger of storms
The pain of suffering
I am the Black Woman

Woman No.3

I have seen the first rain
And the last fire
I am the seasoner of souls
I have many tales untold

Woman No. 4

My womb has been stretched
across the mouth of the universe
To create rhythms and nations
My body has borne witness to birth
My spirit the taster of death

Woman No. 1

I have seen the 13th month
The 32nd day
The year 3000 before the year 03

I have cradled the newborn's cry
Yours and mine
Collected the old man's moan
Made diamonds out of stone
Found gold in my soul

All Women speaking in unison

I am the right hand of God
The equal part of Man
The spirit of Life
I am the Black Woman

NATURAL TO THE BONE!

Music interlude with African drummers. End of play.

ABOUT THE POET

SHIRLEY BRADLEY LEFLORE is an oral poet/performance artist and retired adjunct professor of women's and ethnic literature. She holds a B.A. in Language Arts and Behavioral Science from Webster University and an M.A. in Psychology from Washington University in St. Louis. She was a National Institute in Minority Mental Health Fellow (NIMH), and is the recipient of Missouri Arts Council and CDCA grants.

An original member of the renowned Black Artists Group (BAG) of St. Louis, LeFlore, who performed her poetry nationally and internationally, has collaborated with dancers and visual artists, and worked alongside some of the music giants of jazz, blues, gospel, spirituals and classical music. She has also worked with woodwind virtuoso J.D. Parran, the New York City-based music group Spirit Stage, and collaborated on Hamiet Bluiet's BBQ Band recordings.

LeFlore's poetry and writings have appeared in many anthologies and magazines, including *Spirit & Flame, Anthology of Contemporary African American Poetry* (1997), *ALOUD: Voices from the Nuyorican Poets Café* (1995), *Black American Literature Forum: Henry Dumas, Vol. 22, No. 2* (1988), *Turn in the River: Celebrate Issue for Gwendolyn Brooks* (1988), and *SHEBA REVIEW: Anthology of Missouri Women Writers* (1987). LeFlore recently published her first poetry collection, *Brassbones & Rainbows,* and the production of her play, *Rivers of Women,* marks the directorial debut of her dauther, bestselling author and producer Lyah Beth LeFlore.

PHOTO CREDIT : Kelly Revelle / Revelle Photography, Crystal City, MO

ABOUT THE PHOTOGRAPHER

MICHAEL J. BRACEY is an award-winning Chicago-based photographer that has lectured and exhibited extensively throughout the United States and abroad. His work has appeared in *The Journey: The Next 100 Years,* a book created and published by the Chicago Alliance of African-American Photographers (CAAAP) in conjunction with Roosevelt University Press, the Chicago History Museum, and the Chicago Tribune newspaper.

His other books are *Urban Waters, People-Places-Peru, The Black Christ Festival of Portobelo (Panama), Ten Days in Morocco, It's All about the Hats,* and *Ten Days in Guatemala.*

Bracey's accomplishments include the CAAAP Portfolio of the Year award (2001), a Chicago Arts Assistant Council grant (2004), a Hutchinson Arts Association Council grant (2004), and the Illinois Arts Council Fellowship (2003) for Africans Within the Americas, a ten-year project of travel to twelve different countries documenting commonalities among people of African descent, which resulted in a traveling exhibition and a book.

Bracey holds a B.A. from Webster University, St. Louis, and a M.A. in Interdisciplinary Arts from Columbia College Chicago. He is a foundation member of CAAAP (founded 1999), where he has served as Vice President, President and Treasurer.◉

ABOUT THE PRODUCER & DIRECTOR

LYAH BETH LEFLORE is a National Bestselling author of seven books and television producer. She has been featured in *The New York Times, Essence Magazine, Ebony, Jet, Entertainment Weekly,* CNN and BET.

Her novels include, *Wildflowers* (2009) and *Last Night A DJ Saved My Life* (2006). She is also the coauthor of the recently published *The Strawberry Letter: Real Talk, Real Advice, Because Bitterness Isn't Sexy* (2011), by Shirley Strawberry, co-host of the Steve Harvey Morning Show, and *Can't Hold Me Down* (2010) by DL Warfield, CEO of Goldfinger.

Having worked as an assistant to the SVP of Programming and Development at Nickelodeon, LeFlore went on to become a producer and executive at major production companies such as Nickelodeon, Uptown Entertainment/Universal, and Alan Haymon Productions, where she served as VP of Development and Production/Producer for ten years. Her producer credits include: *New York Undercover* (FOX – Wolf Films/Universal), *Midnight Mac* starring Bernie Mac (HBO), and *Grown Ups* (UPN). LeFlore currently serves as as Creator/Writer/Producer of the hot webseries *8 Days a Week* based on *The Come Up* for BET Networks' BET.com.

In 2013 LeFlore directed and executive produced the stage play *Rivers of Women,* a musical choreopoem written by and based on poems by her mother, acclaimed poet and performing artist, Shirley Bradley LeFlore, at the Missouri History Museum's 2012-2013 theater season.

LeFlore, a native of St. Louis, Missouri, holds a B.A. in Communications Media from Stephens College, and is also a member of the Alpha Kappa Alpha Sorority Incorporated. She actively speaks on the lecture circuit and continues to work on various literary, television, film and theatrical projects. For more information on LeFlore, go to www.greenleflore.com. ©

THE CREATIVE TEAM

EDWARD CURTIS, III: Executive Producer

EDWARD CURTIS, III is a businessman and real estate developer. Having developed both commercial and residential properties, Curtis began his career in advertising, founding Curtis Company, a full service advertising agency from 1970–1993 when he sold the company to H.A.L.O. Industries. He went on to create Curtis Distribution Company, and simultaneously managed 2 PGA Tour Players. Curtis struck gold again recently when he opened St. Louis' premiere steak house, Prime 1000. Currently, Curtis has expanded his role as a businessman into the world of entertainment and is one of the Executive Producers of *3 Nights In August,* starring Academy Award Winner, Billy Bob Thornton.

Curtis, a native of Mt. Vernon, Ill, currently resides in St Louis. He holds a B.S. from University of Emporia, Kansas, a M.S. from Southern Illinois University-Carbondale, and attended C.A.S., Advertising Specialty Institute. ◉

TAKIA "TIZZI" GREEN: Executive Producer

TAKIA "TIZZI" GREEN'S ascension began in 1997 when she was one of seven individuals handpicked out of thousands by Lions Gate CEO, Jon Feltheimer, the then EVP of Sony Pictures Entertainment and President of Columbia Tri-Star TV. Green soared in the Jon Feltheimer Diversity Mentorship program for Sony/Columbia Tri-Star Pictures when she worked above and beyond her duties of a production assistant on the CBS television series, The Gregory Hines Show, composing three original songs for the program. She went on to work with top music concert promoter and Executive Producer Alan Haymon, working as production assistant, writer's assistant, and eventually executive assistant to Haymon and producer, Lyah Beth LeFlore. During her tenure, she worked on multiple television shows, such as UPN's *Grown Up's* and *Out of Bounds,* among others.

On the music front, she has become a go-to songwriter and producer, working with music heavyweights like multi-platinum producer Darryl "Dok" Ross, YoYo, Kurtis Blow; and R&B legends Kool And The Gang, to name a few. Green is a producing partner with LeFlore, for their companies Majestic 9 Films LLC and Dolly's Girls Productions. She also serves as a producer on the hot new scripted original web series *8 Days A Week* for BET Network that airs on BET.com. She recently penned her first short film *Bully Me No More,* and is currently writing her first feature script entitled "The Battle Within." ◉

MARSHA CANN: Producer

MARSHA CANN, a St. Louis native, is well-known as an actress, poet, storyteller and educator. Her work has been published in *Wordwalkers, Frontlines* and *St. Louis Muse.* Cann has often been seen on stage in productions with the St. Louis Black Rep., an association that dates back to the origins of the company when she was a theater major at Washington University. For seven years, Cann lived in New York City, where she began teaching creative writing and drama in afterschool programs in the public schools and performing poetry in showcase and jazz venues.

For over 22 years, she has worked in education and performing arts in the St. Louis area. She currently works with the Young Artists for Justice & Peace, serving as artistic director for their 40 Corners street theatre project.◉

ALERICA ANDERSON: Composer/Producer

ALERICA ANDERSON is a consummate singer, songwriter, composer, producer and director. Born in St. Louis, Missouri, he spent his childhood surrounded by great performers and musicians. He began playing in churches at the age of twelve. As a Music Performance Major at the University of Missouri-Columbia, Anderson studied jazz and music performance and directed the University's Gospel Choir. While continuing his studies at Southern Illinois University at Edwardsville, he was asked and became an adjunct faculty member in the music department of Southern Illinois University at Edwardsville; he later served in the same capacity at St. Louis Community College at Florissant Valley.

In the mid-1990s, Anderson left his teaching position and began his career as a songwriter and performer, working as Music Director/Keyboardist for several touring and local artists. He has been Music Director for several theatrical productions including *The Tap Dance Kid* (St.Louis Black Repertory Company), productions with Historyonics Theatre Co., Liberty Playhouse, and several Collegiate Productions (University of Missouri-Columbia, Southern Illinois University at Edwardsville).

Anderson has performed with both secular and gospel artists including: Edwin Hawkins, Walter Hawkins, David Peaston, The Drifters, Melba Moore, Lynn Whitfield, Dr Bobby Jones, The Ebony Fashion Fair, The Miss Universe Pageant and Celine Dion. He also serves as Director of Music for the First Baptist Church of Chesterfield, in St. Louis. He has also written and produced songs for various gospel and secular recordings, including the Edwin and Walter Hawkins Music and Arts Seminar Mass Choir. He recently completed his debut worship album as Alerica Anderson and The Voices of Jesus Christ, entitled *I Love You Lord*. His production credits also include "PeaceFest," an outdoor concert event held annually in St. Louis. ◉

PHOTO CREDIT : Tyrone Nathan Turner Photography

NICOLE "PINKY" THOMAS: Choreographer

NICOLE "PINKY" THOMAS is highly respected in the dance industry as a performer, instructor, choreographer and humanitarian. A native of University City, Missouri, Nicole is a graduate of Central Visual & Performing Arts High School in St. Louis and received her B.F.A. in dance from The University of Illinois Champaign-Urbana. Introduced to ballet and tap as a young child and quickly became a member of the award winning Ray Parks Academy of Dance Competition Team. As an adolescent, Nicole began training in Dunham Technique at the Katherine Dunham Center for the Performing Arts, S.I.U.E., and East St. Louis Center under the direction of Theodore Jamison. Over the years she expanded her knowledge of dance by studying African, Caribbean, Haitian, Cuban, Capoeira, and yoga techniques.

Thomas has traveled throughout the U.S. and Europe, working with companies across the country, including the world renowned Katherine Dunham Dance Ensemble – SIUE, Martha Graham Dance Company, Urban Bush Women, The MUNY, Jose Limon Dance Company, Spirit of Angela West African Dance Ensemble, Inner Vision Dance Theatre, CounterGroove Dance Company, Minianka African Drum & Dance Ensemble, and Banyan Dance Theater.

She has appeared in countless stage productions including *A Chorus Line, Three Coins in the Fountain, Showboat,* and *Tap Dance Kid,* and has staged musicals across the country such as *Fiddler on the Roof, Once Upon this Island, The Wiz,* and *Children of Eden.* Thomas has held workshops and has ongoing residencies with the Missouri Historical Society, Kaatsbaan International Dance Center, Inc., Stages St. Louis-Education Outreach, Girls Scouts of Eastern Missouri, St. Louis Public Schools, International Association of Blacks in Dance, Black College Dance Exchange, Neighborhood Houses, Club CHIPS, and many more. In 2006, she founded the Pinx Academy of Dance in University City, where she offers a comprehensive dance curriculum to students and professionals of all ages. ☺

THERESA ANDERSON: Associate Producer

THERESA ANDERSON, native of Saint Louis, MO is proud to be a part of a creative and inspiring endeavor, *Rivers of Women* by her aunt, Shirley Bradley LeFlore. Having spent a major part of her life exposed to LeFlore's poetry and performances, taking part in this production is a lifetime opportunity. Anderson has successfully managed and directed multiple projects and tasks in both the corporate environment and local communities. She is a forward thinking, resourceful, compassionate and highly creative professional with a consistent record of success meeting and exceeding goals in complex surroundings. ◉

PHOTO CREDITS

SUITE I: THE SPIRIT
"Give Me Rivers" p. 1
> Shirley LeFlore / 2011 / St Louis, MO / performance of "Rivers of Women" / Photo Credit: Michael J. Bracey
> Photo of MeMe / The LeFlore Family Collection

"Woman I Am" p. 2
> Untitled / 2012 / Chicago, IL / Photo Credit: Michael J. Bracey

"The Women Gather" p. 3
> The Neals women / Michigan / Neals-Muhammad Wedding / Photo Credit: Michael J. Bracey
> Untitled / Michigan / Neals-Muhammad Wedding / Photo Credit: Michael J. Bracey

"I Have Known Women" p. 7
> (collage of six) / 2010 /Chicago, IL / exhibition and book, *It's all about the Hats* / Photo Credit: Michael J. Bracey
> Woman on Maxwell Street / 1997 / Chicago, IL / Photo Credit: Michael J. Bracey
> Guatemalan grandmother / 2011 / Antigua, Guatemala / *Ten Days in Guatemala* / Photo Credit: Michael J. Bracey
> Untitled / 2006 / Taxco, Mexico / Photo Credit: Michael J. Bracey
> Untitled / 2003 / Salvador de Bahia, Brazil / exhibition and book, *Africans Within the Americas* /
>   Photo Credit: Michael J. Bracey
> Silhouette of Shavonne / 1998 / Chicago, IL / Photo Credit: Michael J. Bracey
> Mom getting hair braided / 2008 / Hutchinson, KS / Photo Credit: Michael J. Bracey

SUITE II: THE SOUL
"We Be Dolly's Girls" p. 20
> Shirley's mother's beautyshop / The LeFlore Family Collection
> Shavonne working at CMB / 2011 / Riverside IL / project, "Hair" / Photo Credit: Michael J. Bracey

"Sistas" p. 24
> Kendra and Rabindra / 2010 / Chicago, IL / exhibition and book, *It's all about the Hats* /
>   Photo Credit: Michael J. Bracey
> Paris and Magoly / 2010 / Chicago, IL / exhibition and book, *It's all about the Hats* /
>   Photo Credit: Michael J. Bracey

PHOTO: Photographer Michael J. Bracey with the poet Shirley Bradley LeFlore, circa 1979 in St. Louis, Missouri. *Photo courtesy of Michael J. Bracey.*

Shavonne and Takeya / 2010 / Chicago, IL / exhibition and book, *It's all about the Hats* /
  Photo Credit: Michael J. Bracey
The Bracey Girls/ 2010 / Hutchinson, KS / exhibition and book, *It's all about the Hats* /
  Photo Credit: Michael J. Bracey

"Wildflowers" p. 28
  Untitled/1995 / Lisle, IL / Photo Credit: Michael J. Bracey
  JoAnn R / 1982 / Hutchinson, KS / Photo Credit: Michael J. Bracey

SUITE III: LOVE
"Quiet Storm (He Came)" p. 33
  Untitled / 1999 / Chicago, IL / project, "Makes me Wanna Holla" / Photo Credit: Michael J. Bracey

"Used To Be" p. 35
  Untitled / 2013 / Chicago, IL / project, The Bracey Family Collection

"I Hear You Comin'" p. 37
  La Luna #3 / 2012 / Chicago, IL / Photo Credit: Michael J. Bracey

"Saturdaynite Houserent" p. 40
  Out on the Town / cir 1948 / Chicago, IL / The Bracey Family Collection
  House partying / cir 1948 / Chicago, IL / project, The Bracey Family Collection

"Men Have Buttered My bread" p. 44
  A.G. / 1989 /Chicago, IL / Photo Credit: Michael J. Bracey

"Put Ya Haints on Me" p. 46
  Photos 1, 2, & 3 / 2011 / St Louis, MO / performance, *Rivers of Women* / Photo Credit: Michael J. Bracey

"Love Poem" p. 56
  Smiling Ghanaian Woman / 1999 / Accra, Ghana / exhibition and book, *Africans Within the Americas* /
  Photo Credit: Michael J. Bracey

SUITE IV: HEALING
"When a Sisterwomanpoet Prays" p. 58
  Untitled / 2003 / Semàna, Dominican Republic / exhibition and book, *Africans Within the Americas* /
  .Photo Credit: Michael J. Bracey

"Time Wise for Me Me" p. 58
Sister Bracey / 2006 / Hutchinson, KS / Photo Credit: Michael J. Bracey
Suebee / 2010 / Bolingbrook, IL / exhibition and book, *It's all about the Hats* / Photo Credit: Michael J. Bracey
Twins / 2009 / Chincha Alta, Peru / exhibition and book, *Africans Within the Americas* /
Photo Credit: Michael J. Bracey
Aunt Peggy turns 100 / 2002/ Chicago, IL / exhibition and book, *Africans Within the Americas* /
Photo Credit: Michael J. Bracey

"Broken N' Parts" p. 65
The Alter / 2012 / Chicago, IL / Photo Credit: Michael J. Bracey

"Healing" p. 68
Untitled / 2013 / Chicago, IL / Photo Credit: Michael J. Bracey

"The Caged Bird Sings" p. 70
Deacon Reynolds / 1982 / Hutchinson, KS / project, "Makes me Wanna Holla"
Untitled / 2003 / Belo Horizonte, Brazil / exhibition and book, *Africans within the Americas*

"I Woke-up This Morning" p. 73
KoKo Taylor at the Rivera / 2000 / Chicago, IL / exhibition and book, *The Journey: The Next 100 Years*
Untitled / 2010 / Chicago, IL / Photo Credit: Michael J. Bracey
Untitled / unknown / The LeFlore Family Collection / Photo Credit: Michael J. Bracey

"The Dancer" p. 77
Untitled / 1989 / Chicago, IL / Photo Credit: Michael J. Bracey

"Poem for a Black Woman" p. 78
Kym at dawn / Chicago, IL / exhibition and book, *Africans Within the Americas* / Photo Credit: Michael J. Bracey
Sheila at dawn / 2011/ Chicago, IL / Photo Credit: Michael J. Bracey
Angela and baby / Chicago, IL / Photo Credit: Michael J. Bracey

OTHER BOOKS BY 2LEAF PRESS

2LEAF PRESS challenges the status quo by publishing alternative fiction, non-fiction, poetry and bilingual works by activists, academics, poets and authors dedicated to diversity and social justice with scholarship that is accessible to the general public. 2LEAF PRESS produces high quality and beautifully produced hardcover, paperback and ebook formats through our series: *2LP Explorations in Diversity, 2LP University Books, 2LP Classics, 2LP Translations, Nuyorican World Series,* and *2LP Current Affairs, Culture & Politics.* Below is a selection of 2LEAF PRESS' published titles.

2LP EXPLORATIONS IN DIVERSITY
Substance of Fire: Gender and Race in the College Classroom
by Claire Millikin
Foreword by R. Joseph Rodríguez, Afterword by Richard Delgado
Contributed material by Riley Blanks, Blake Calhoun, Rox Trujillo

Black Lives Have Always Mattered, A Collection of Essays, Poems, and Personal Narratives
Edited by Abiodun Oyewole

The Beiging of America: Personal Narratives about Being Mixed Race in the 21st Century
Edited by Cathy J. Schlund-Vials, Sean Frederick Forbes, Tara Betts
with an Afterword by Heidi Durrow

What Does it Mean to be White in America? Breaking the White Code of Silence, A Collection of Personal Narratives
Edited by Gabrielle David and Sean Frederick Forbes
Introduction by Debby Irving and Afterword by Tara Betts

2LP UNIVERSITY BOOKS
Designs of Blackness, Mappings in the Literature and Culture of African Americans
A. Robert Lee
20TH ANNIVERSARY EXPANDED EDITION

2LP CLASSICS
Adventures in Black and White, Edited and with a critical introduction by Tara Betts
by Philippa Duke Schuyler

Monsters: Mary Shelley's Frankenstein and Mathilda
by Mary Shelley, edited by Claire Millikin Raymond

2LP TRANSLATIONS

Birds on the Kiswar Tree
by Odi Gonzales, Translated by Lynn Levin
Bilingual: English/Spanish

Incessant Beauty, A Bilingual Anthology
by Ana Rossetti, Edited and Translated by Carmela Ferradáns
Bilingual: English/Spanish

NUYORICAN WORLD SERIES

Our Nuyorican Thing, The Birth of a Self-Made Identity
by Samuel Carrion Diaz, with an Introduction by Urayoán Noel
Bilingual: English/Spanish

Hey Yo! Yo Soy!, 40 Years of Nuyorican Street Poetry, The Collected Works of Jesús Papoleto Meléndez
Bilingual: English/Spanish

LITERARY NONFICTION

No Vacancy; Homeless Women in Paradise
by Michael Reid

The Beauty of Being, A Collection of Fables, Short Stories & Essays
by Abiodun Oyewole

WHEREABOUTS: Stepping Out of Place, An Outside in Literary & Travel Magazine Anthology
Edited by Brandi Dawn Henderson

PLAYS

Rivers of Women, The Play
by Shirley Bradley LeFlore, with photographs by Michael J. Bracey

AUTOBIOGRAPHIES/MEMOIRS/BIOGRAPHIES

Trailblazers, Black Women Who Helped Make America Great, American Firsts/American Icons
by Gabrielle David

Mother of Orphans, The True and Curious Story of Irish Alice, A Colored Man's Widow
by Dedria Humphries Barker

Strength of Soul
by Naomi Raquel Enright

Dream of the Water Children: Memory and Mourning in the Black Pacific
by Fredrick D. Kakinami Cloyd
Foreword by Velina Hasu Houston, Introduction by Gerald Horne
Edited by Karen Chau

The Fourth Moment: Journeys from the Known to the Unknown, A Memoir
by Carole J. Garrison, Introduction by Sarah Willis

POETRY

PAPOLíTICO, Poems of a Political Persuasion
by Jesús Papoleto Meléndez
with an Introduction by Joel Kovel and DeeDee Halleck

Critics of Mystery Marvel, Collected Poems
by Youssef Alaoui, with an Introduction by Laila Halaby

shrimp
by jason vasser-elong, with an Introduction by Michael Castro
The Revlon Slough, New and Selected Poems
by Ray DiZazzo, with an Introduction by Claire Millikin

Written Eye: Visuals/Verse
by A. Robert Lee

A Country Without Borders: Poems and Stories of Kashmir
by Lalita Pandit Hogan, with an Introduction by Frederick Luis Aldama

Branches of the Tree of Life, The Collected Poems of Abiodun Oyewole 1969-2013
by Abiodun Oyewole, edited by Gabrielle David
with an Introduction by Betty J. Dopson

2Leaf Press is an imprint owned and operated by the Intercultural Alliance of Artists & Scholars, Inc. (IAAS), a NY-based nonprofit organization that publishes and promotes multicultural literature.

NEW YORK
www.2leafpress.org

"A woman in harmony with her spirit is like a river flowing. She goes where she will without pretense and arrives at her destination prepared to be herself, and only herself."

—Maya Angelou